THE TALE OF TALL TOOTHBRUSH

ELAYNE REISS-WEIMANN
RITA FRIEDMAN

New
Dimensions
in
Education

Home of the Letter People

61 Mattatuck Heights • Waterbury, CT 06705

Copyright© in this format 1990 New Dimensions in Education, Inc.

All rights reserved.

No part of this publication may be reproduced, stored in a retrieval system, or transmitted, in any form or by any means, electronic, mechanical, photocopying, recording, or otherwise, without the prior written permission of the publishers.

Printed in U.S.A.

Hardcover ISBN 0-89796-924-3   12451 (Hardcover)
Softcover ISBN 0-89796-219-2   12520 (Softcover)

3 4 5 6 7 8 9   SPC   SPC   9 8 7 6 5 4 3 2

Every morning Mr. T waits for his friend Tall Toothbrush.
Mr. T loves to have Tall Toothbrush take care of his tall teeth.

1

"Good morning, Mr. T," says Tall Toothbrush happily.
"I will be ready to work
as soon as I set up my equipment."
Mr. T can hardly wait.

At last Tall Toothbrush is ready to begin.
He brushes a tooth from the top of the tip
to the tip of the top.
Then Tall Toothbrush stops.
He tells Mr. T a funny story.
Then he starts brushing another tooth.
The two friends have fun together.

Tall Toothbrush works
and tells Mr. T funny stories.
Mr. T laughs and laughs.
Every morning he laughs so loud,
he wakes up the roosters.
The roosters crow.
They wake up everyone in Letter People Land.
This is the way each day begins.

One day something terrible happens.
It starts when a salesperson introduces
Mr. T to Battery Toothbrush.
Battery Toothbrush shows Mr. T
how fast he can clean Mr. T's tall teeth.
Mr. T likes how quickly Battery Toothbrush works.

The next morning, Tall Toothbrush comes to brush
Mr. T's teeth.
"Wait!" says Mr. T.
"Do not set up your equipment.
You take too much time to clean my teeth.
This is Battery Toothbrush.
From now on he will take care of my teeth.
I do not need you anymore."

Tall Toothbrush is terribly unhappy.

He and Mr. T have been friends for a long time.

Tall Toothbrush loves Mr. T.

What will Tall Toothbrush do?

The next morning, Tall Toothbrush does not come
to Mr. T's house.
Battery Toothbrush brushes Mr. T's tall teeth.
Battery Toothbrush works so fast,
he has no time to tell Mr. T funny stories.
Now the trouble starts
in Letter People Land.
Battery Toothbrush does not make Mr. T laugh.
Mr. T's laughter does not wake up the roosters.
The roosters do not wake up the people.
Everyone is late.

Day after day, Battery Toothbrush quickly
brushes Mr. T's tall teeth.
Mr. T says, "Battery Toothbrush works
much faster than Tall Toothbrush.
Battery Toothbrush cleans my teeth quickly,
but I never laugh anymore."

One day, Battery Toothbrush cannot work.
He tells Mr. T he needs new batteries.
Mr. T looks at the clock.
He says, "The stores should be open now.
I will go and buy batteries."

Mr. T goes from store to store.

The stores are closed.

There are no people in the streets.

There are no cars.

There are no buses.

Mr. T does not understand.

Then he sees the roosters sleeping.

"Wake up," he calls.

"Why are you still sleeping?"

"There is no one to awaken us,"
answer the roosters.

"You never laugh anymore."

Mr. T says, "It is true I never laugh anymore.
I should never have sent Tall Toothbrush away.
He did more than just brush my teeth.
He made me happy.
I did not treat him right.
I must tell him I was wrong."

Mr. T telephones Tall Toothbrush.
There is no answer.
Mr. T goes to Tall Toothbrush's house.
Tall Toothbrush is not there.
Mr. T looks everywhere for Tall Toothbrush.
He cannot find him.
Mr. T says, "I must find Tall Toothbrush.
I must tell him I'm sorry.
I have an idea."

In a place far away,

Tall Toothbrush turns on a television set.

He sees Mr. T.

He hears Mr. T say,

"I want everyone to know

that the trouble in Letter People Land is all my fault.

I had a very good friend.

He cared about me.

I sent him away.

I am sorry.

If Tall Toothbrush is listening,

I hope he will forgive me."

Every day, Mr. T waits and watches for Tall Toothbrush.

Battery Toothbrush waits and watches too.

He is tired of cleaning Mr. T's tall teeth.

He uses up too many batteries.

For a long time, Tall Toothbrush does not come.

Then one morning, Mr. T sees something.

He thinks he is dreaming.

He rushes to the door.

There is Tall Toothbrush carrying his equipment.

The next morning the roosters are sleeping.
Suddenly they hear Mr. T laughing.
Happily, the roosters crow.
Everyone in Letter People Land wakes up.
The day begins!